SPACE

ADVENTURE

WIDE EYED EDITIONS

ARE YOU READY TO MAKE THE BEST STORIES EVER?

HERE'S HOW IT WORKS:

READ THE QUESTION AT THE TOP OF THE PAGE.

CHOOSE SOMETHING FROM THE PICTURES TO HELP YOU TELL YOUR STORY.

TALK ABOUT THE CHOICES YOU'VE MADE IN AS MUCH DETAIL AS YOU CAN.

HERE ARE SOME THINGS YOU COULD THINK ABOUT. LOOK OUT FOR MORE ON EACH PAGE.

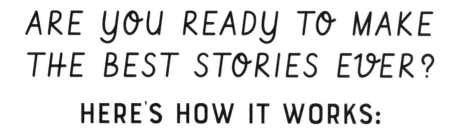

YOU'RE ABOUT TO GO ON AN ADVENTURE. WHICH ONE OF THESE HEROES DO YOU WANT TO BE?

A princess

An alien

An armadillo

An astronaut

A clown

An explorer

A scientist

A dinosaur

An artist

DESCRIBE THE CHARACTERS. ARE THEY HAPPY? GRUMPY? SAD? TALL? SHORT? KIND? MEAN?

WHAT CAN YOU SEE, HEAR, AND SMELL AROUND YOU?

DO YOU TALK TO ANY OF THE CHARACTERS? WHAT DO THEIR VOICES SOUND LIKE?

WHAT'S THE WEATHER LIKE?

TELL IT OUT LOUD, MAKE IT UP IN YOUR HEAD, OR WRITE IT DOWN ON A PIECE OF PAPER.

CREATE THE STORY HOWEVER YOU LIKE! YOU COULD ALSO ADD ANY EXTRA CHOICES OR STORY ELEMENTS THAT YOU WANT.

WHEN YOU'VE FINISHED, COME BACK TO THE START AND BEGIN A COMPLETELY NEW TALE. THERE ARE MILLIONS (THAT'S RIGHT—MILLIONS!) OF DIFFERENT STORIES THAT CAN BE MADE WITH THIS BOOK.

HOW MANY CAN YOU TELL?

IT'S TIME TO START THE ADVENTURE.
3... 2... 1... LET'S TELL A STORY!

GOOD LUCK!
I'M COMING TOO! SPOT ME HIDING THROUGH THE BOOK.

YOU'RE ABOUT TO GO ON AN ADVENTURE.
WHICH ONE OF THESE HEROES DO YOU WANT TO BE?

A princess

An alien

An armadillo

An astronaut

An explorer

A scientist

A clown

An artist

A dinosaur

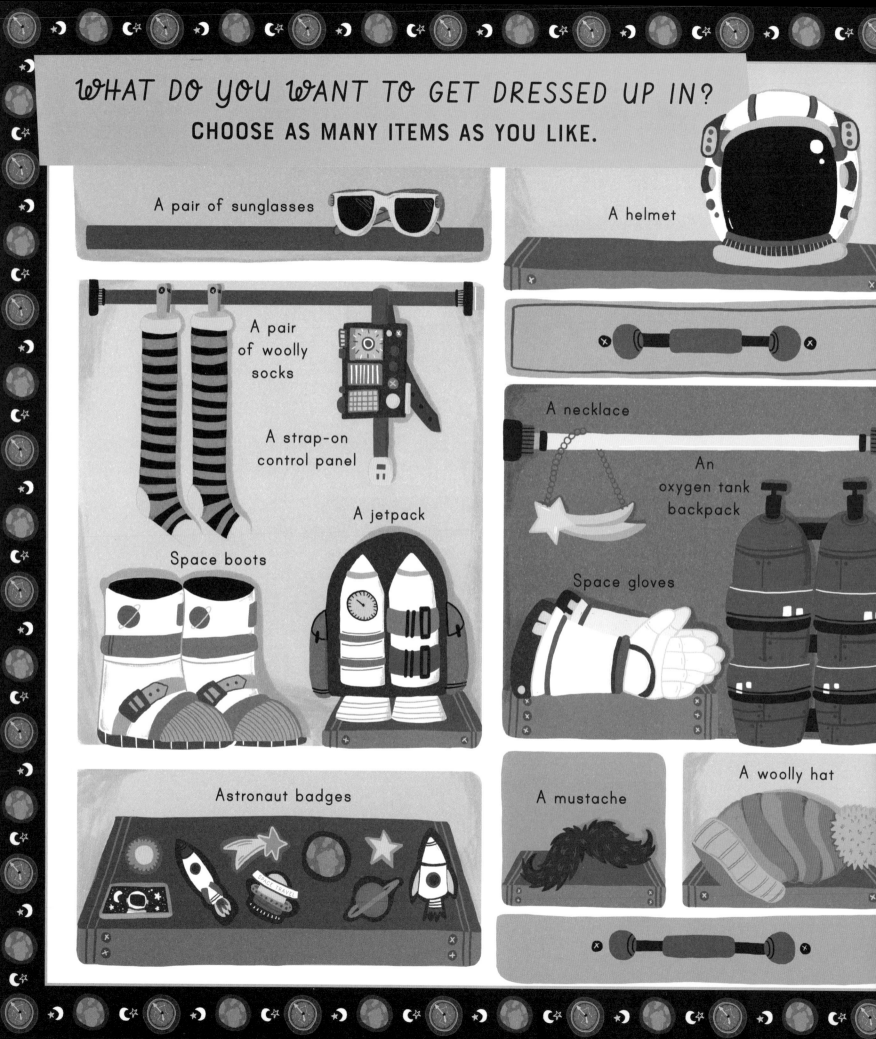

WHAT DO YOU WANT TO GET DRESSED UP IN?
CHOOSE AS MANY ITEMS AS YOU LIKE.

A pair of sunglasses

A helmet

A pair of woolly socks

A strap-on control panel

A jetpack

Space boots

A necklace

An oxygen tank backpack

Space gloves

Astronaut badges

A mustache

A woolly hat

SPACE TRAVEL

WHERE DO YOU WANT TO GO?
CHOOSE A PLACE TO VISIT.

A planet made of sushi

Jupiter

The brightest star in the sky

A planet made of gold

To the man on the moon

Planet Cheese

A galaxy of singing stars

Unicorn planet

WHAT DO YOU NEED TO TAKE WITH YOU?
YOU HAVE ROOM IN YOUR BAG FOR THREE THINGS.

A family photo

Space food

A toothbrush and toothpaste

A flashlight

Water

A pet rock

Space plants

WHAT MIGHT YOU NEED THEM FOR?

A crafting kit

A map of the stars

Equipment for experiments

A guitar

A sleeping bag

A teddy

Some juggling balls

Your favorite books

A diary

A hot water bottle

Some paints and paper

An asteroid collecting kit

An alarm clock

Some sleeping masks

A bag for space travel sickness

A camera

A music player

A flag

A telescope

YOU'RE PACKED AND ALMOST READY TO GO. BUT IT COULD GET LONELY IN SPACE...
TURN THE PAGE TO CHOOSE YOUR CREW.

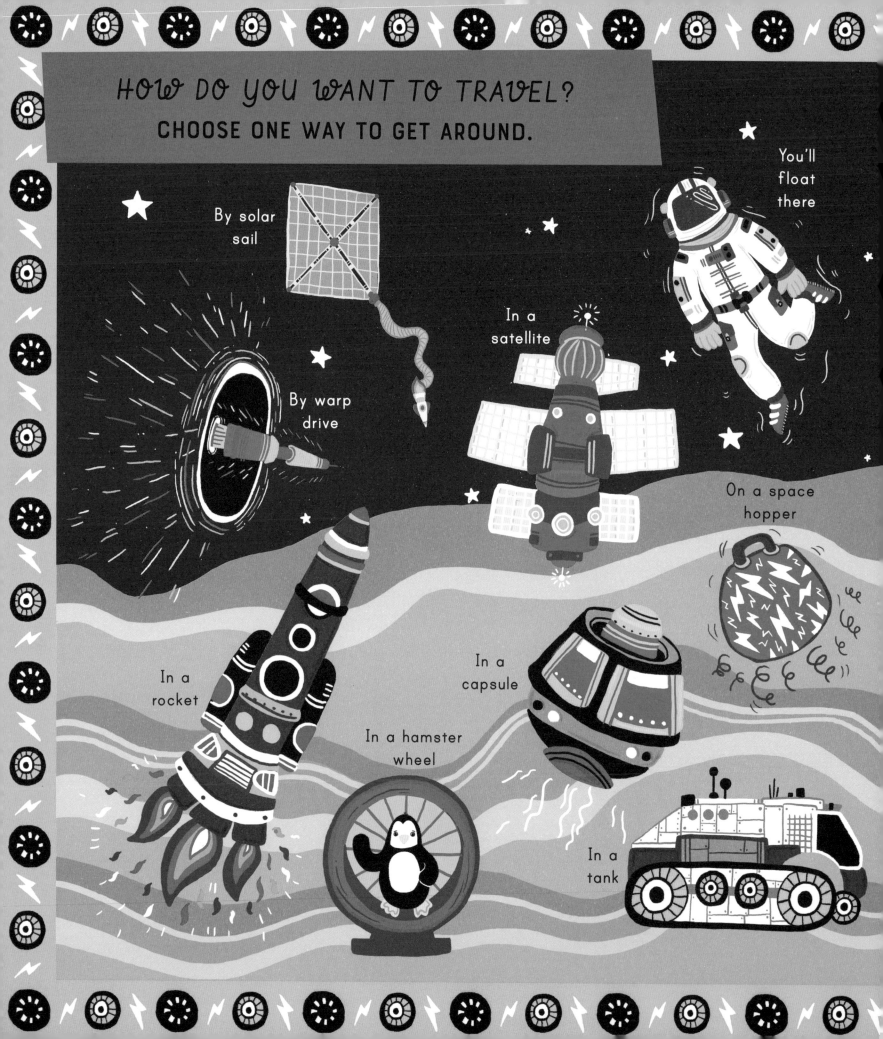

NOW IT'S TIME TO MAP OUT YOUR ROUTE.
PLAN YOUR PATH AND WHAT YOU SEE ON THE WAY.

Whichever way
is the fastest!

Through the Milky Way

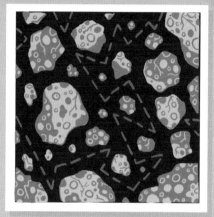

Zig-zagging through
the asteroid belt

WHAT DO YOUR
CREW GET UP TO ON
THE JOURNEY?

Past the Magician Moon

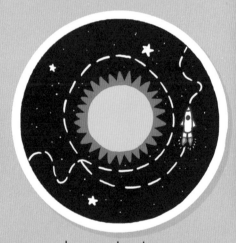

Loop-the-loop
around the Sun

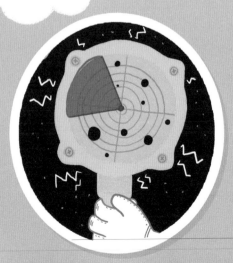

You'll follow the
sounds of alien life

DEEP SPACE
THIS WAY

Straight into
Deep Space

Galaxy hopping

WHAT HAPPENS ALONG THE WAY?

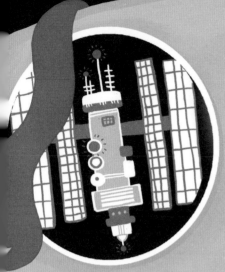

Past a
space station

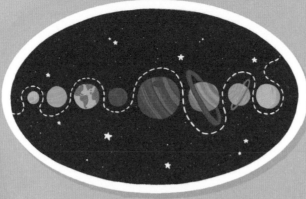

Round each of the planets
in the Solar System

You'll follow the path
of a comet

You don't plan—you'll
get there just fine!

Through the Swamp of
Tentacled Monsters

Past the Universe
of Cats

Through a swirling
space storm

Zooming past
Planet Chocolate

WHAT AN AMAZING TRIP! IS
SOMEONE THERE TO GREET
YOU WHEN YOU ARRIVE?
TURN THE PAGE TO FIND OUT.

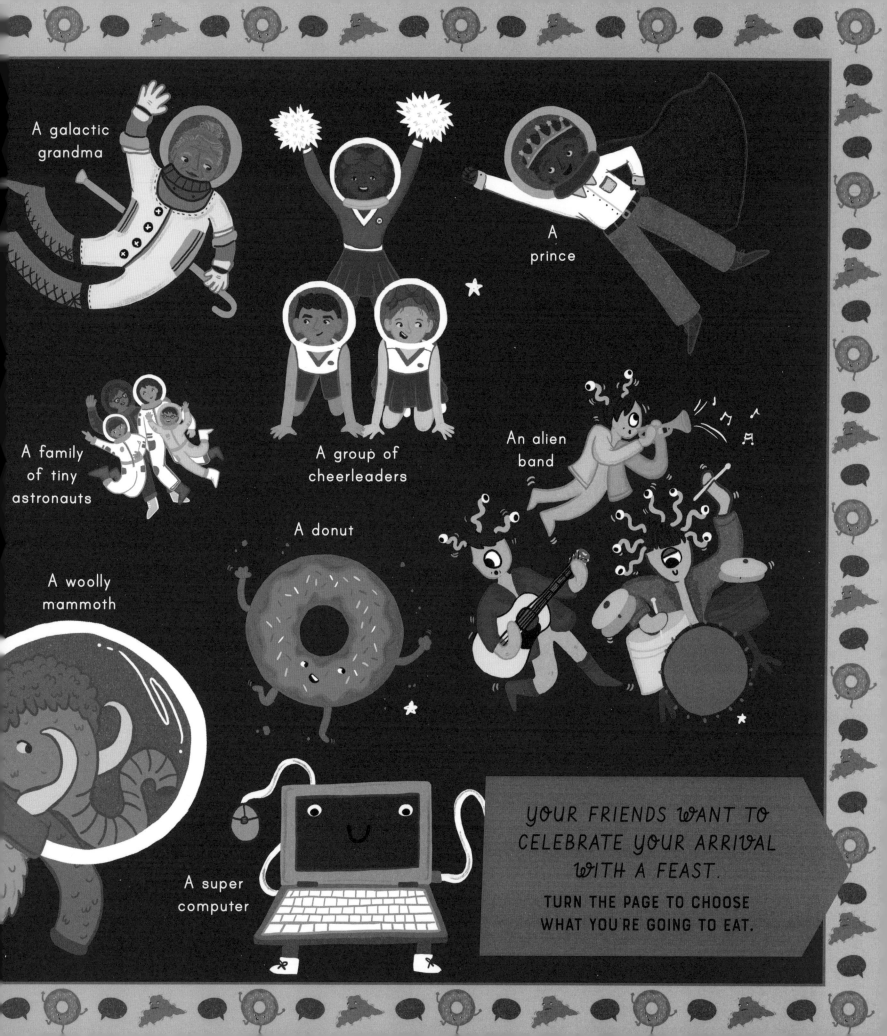

A galactic grandma

A prince

A family of tiny astronauts

A group of cheerleaders

An alien band

A woolly mammoth

A donut

A super computer

YOUR FRIENDS WANT TO CELEBRATE YOUR ARRIVAL WITH A FEAST.

TURN THE PAGE TO CHOOSE WHAT YOU'RE GOING TO EAT.

WHAT WILL YOU EAT AT THE SPACE FEAST?
FILL YOUR PLATE WITH WHATEVER YOU'D LIKE.

Rocket popsicles

Stellar sandwiches

Earth cookies

Rock candy

A surprise dish

Martian meatballs

Asteroid soup

Moon fries

Ice cream SUNdae

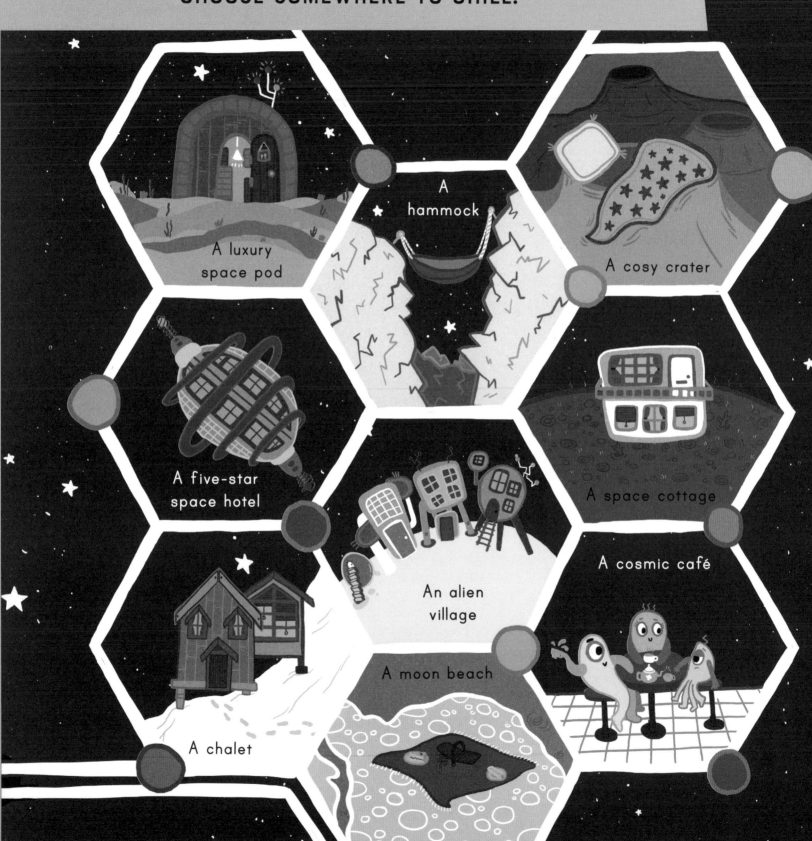

A luxury space pod

A hammock

A cosy crater

A five-star space hotel

A space cottage

An alien village

A cosmic café

A chalet

A moon beach

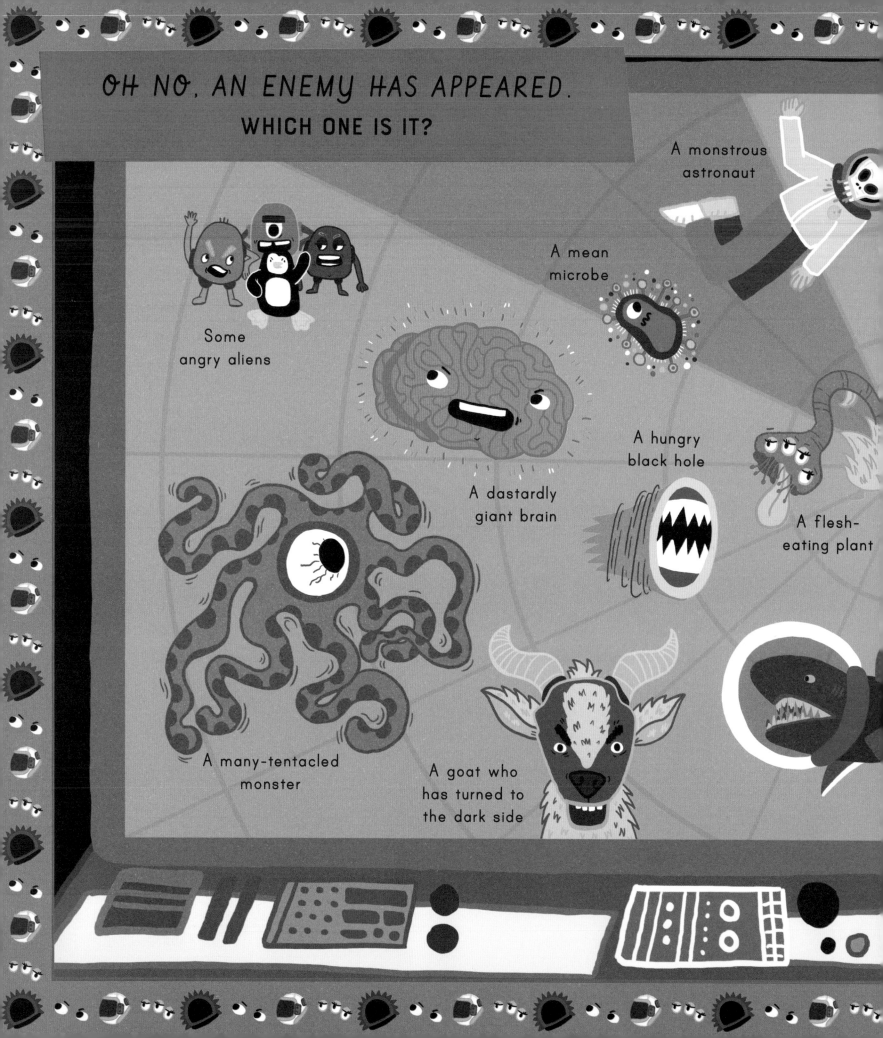

YES, THERE'S A WAY OUT OF DANGER!
WHICH ONE WILL YOU CHOOSE?

You splatter your
enemy with a gloop gun

You freeze
everything
around you

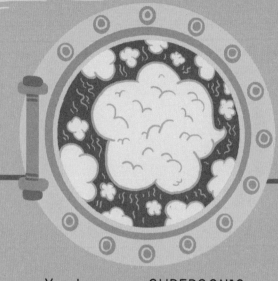

You let out a SUPERSONIC
fart and blast your
enemy away

You agree to
part peacefully

You find a super-fast
jetpack and blast off

You cause a distraction
with some magic tricks

You bribe your
enemy with precious
space gems

You dive through a worm
hole to a parallel universe

You hide in a crater until the danger has passed

You hitch a ride on a shooting star

You summon an incredible storm

You jump in a nearby rocket and warp to safety

You're saved by a space dragon

You dress up as an alien and make loud beeping noises

A friend comes to your rescue

You quickly tunnel underground

DESCRIBE YOUR DARING ESCAPE.

YOU AND YOUR CREW ESCAPE!

WHAT'S YOUR REWARD? CHOOSE ONE OVER THE PAGE.

WHAT'S YOUR REWARD?

PICK ONE PRIZE TO KEEP.

Intergalactic
fame

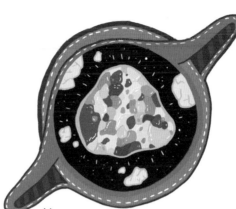

Your very
own meteorite

A brand new
space suit

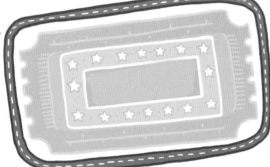

A ticket for a
space cruise

Superblaster
skates

Alien friends for life

A translator to teach
you every alien language

A free journey
to anywhere in
outer space

The biggest gem
in the universe

A time machine

WHAT DO
YOU DO WITH
YOUR REWARD?

A pet snail

All the secrets that
have ever existed

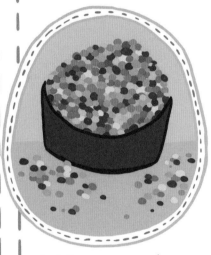

A lifetime supply
of space sweets

A net full of stars to
hang in your bedroom

A ladder to space

A pair of
magic socks

YOUR ADVENTURE
IS NEARLY OVER.
THERE'S JUST ONE MORE
DECISION TO MAKE OVER THE PAGE.

WHAT HAPPENS NEXT?
CHOOSE AN ENDING FOR YOUR TALE.

You write a bestselling book about your adventures

You open a hotel on Mars

You set off on your next adventure

You set up a hair salon on Venus

You get invited to an alien wedding

You go home and never set foot in space again

You get to meet a space queen

You set up a school for astronauts

You star in your own
space movie

You take a relaxing vacation

You discover
a new planet

You decide to become
a jungle explorer

You have a party
to celebrate

You become rich beyond
your wildest dreams

You build a new,
super-fast spacecraft

You drink a potion and turn
yourself into an alien

YOU'VE TOLD A BRILLIANT STORY.
GOOD LUCK ON ALL YOUR FUTURE ADVENTURES!

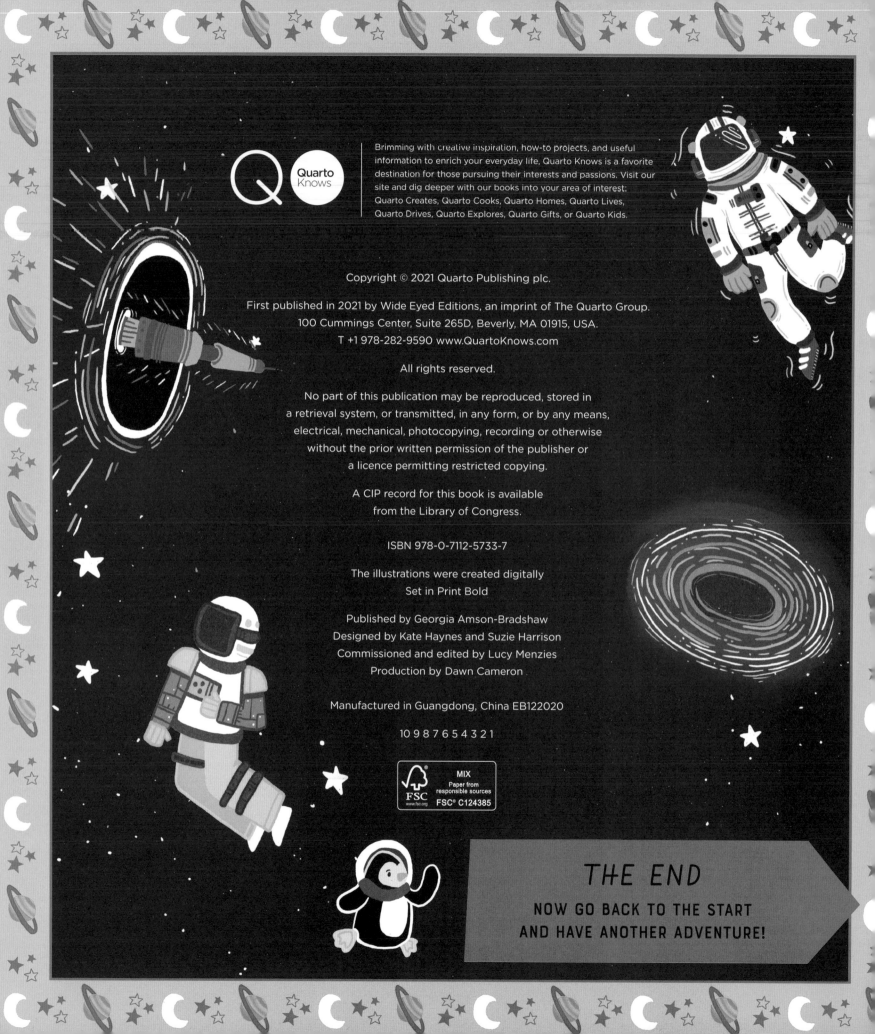

Quarto Knows

Brimming with creative inspiration, how-to projects, and useful information to enrich your everyday life, Quarto Knows is a favorite destination for those pursuing their interests and passions. Visit our site and dig deeper with our books into your area of interest: Quarto Creates, Quarto Cooks, Quarto Homes, Quarto Lives, Quarto Drives, Quarto Explores, Quarto Gifts, or Quarto Kids.

First published in 2021 by Wide Eyed Editions, an imprint of The Quarto Group.
100 Cummings Center, Suite 265D, Beverly, MA 01915, USA.
T +1 978-282-9590 www.QuartoKnows.com

ISBN 978-0-7112-5733-7

The illustrations were created digitally
Set in Print Bold

Published by Georgia Amson-Bradshaw
Designed by Kate Haynes and Suzie Harrison
Commissioned and edited by Lucy Menzies
Production by Dawn Cameron

Manufactured in Guangdong, China EB122020

10 9 8 7 6 5 4 3 2 1

FSC
MIX
Paper from responsible sources
www.fsc.org FSC® C124385

THE END

NOW GO BACK TO THE START
AND HAVE ANOTHER ADVENTURE!

I HAVE A NAME

The Story Of A Pug Named Cass

Carlos Montoya

Illustrated by
Amy Meyer Allen

ISBN: 9781790527830

First printing December 2018

Early on an ordinary Tuesday morning,
a little pug named Cass was ready to
eat breakfast.

Cass was different than most dogs. He loved
broccoli and spinach mixed in scrambled eggs.
He even liked chia seeds sprinkled on top!

Sometimes Cass wanted his mom,
Stephanie, to add some whole cream but that
rarely happened. But when it did, it was wa,
wa, wonderful! "Woof! Woof!"

After gobbling his meal, Cass looked up at
Stephanie with big, brown eyes. He pretended
to still be hungry. "No more Cass or I'll have to
roll you out the door!" she said.

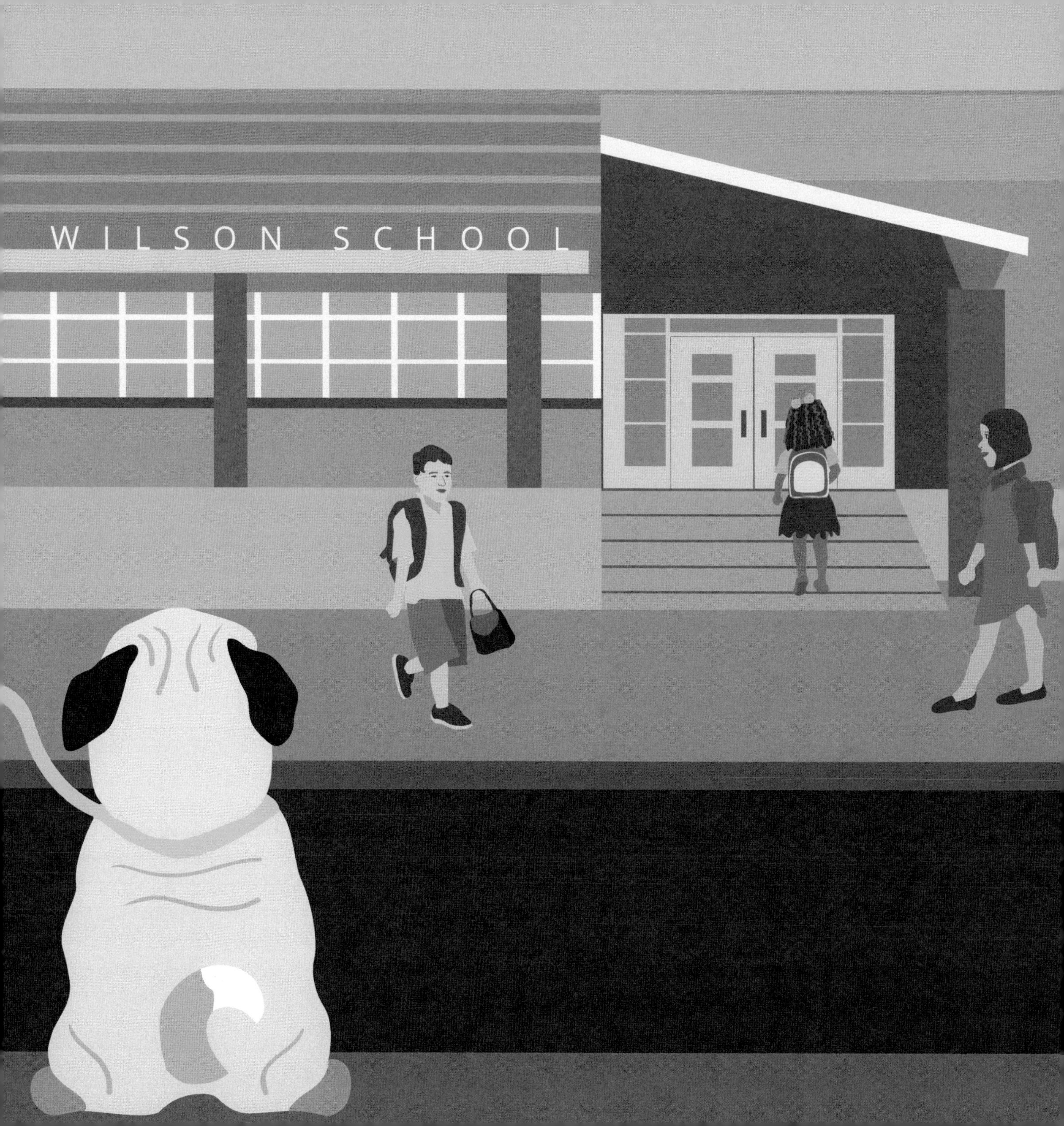
WILSON SCHOOL

As Stephanie reached for his leash and harness, Cass jumped for joy. He loved walks!

"Cass! Hold still. I can't be late for work!" Stephanie exclaimed. Once Cass settled down she put on his harness, attached the leash, grabbed the house keys and off they went.

As always they walked out the apartment door turned left, down the hallway and out the front door of their apartment complex. Soon they joined the children crossing the street to Wilson Elementary School.

Cass knew the way like the back of his paw. He had walked it a thousand times.

Cass loved his walks, but there was always one thing that upset him. No one ever called him by his name.

They always said things like:

"Oh, look at the cute little pug!"

"Mommy, can I get a doggie like that?"

"What a sweet puppy!"

Every day it was the same thing. They would talk about Cass as if he had no name.

It made Cass feel sad, but he got used to it.

At the school crossing, Cass saw a big, black car zooming toward the intersection. It was going very, very fast. Cass knew the cars slowed down for the kids as Mr. Johnson, the crossing guard, guided them across the street. But this car wasn't slowing down!

"Oh no, something bad is going to happen," Cass worried.

Mr. Johnson waved the STOP sign. He blew his whistle as loud as he could!

The big black car was not slowing down. Suddenly Cass saw something that made him very afraid.

Right behind Mr. Johnson, in the path of the speeding car was a little girl with yellow shoes, a polka dot dress and a blue backpack almost as big as her. She had slipped away from her mother and was crossing the street.

Her mother screamed, "Help!" My little girl!"

Cass knew something had to be done! The speeding car was getting very close. Just as Mr. Johnson reached out to grab the little girl, he tripped and fell against the curb.

Cass sprang into action. He pulled away from his mom and ran as fast as his little legs would carry him.

Stephanie yelled, "CASS, COME BACK!"

Cass heard his mother's cries, but he knew he had a job to do. He ran faster than he ever had before.

As he reached the curb, he jumped as high as he could and flew through the air toward the little girl. With all the might in his little 17 pound body, he pushed her away from harm.

They tumbled onto the sidewalk. As the car whizzed by, the little girl's mother scooped her into her arms. "Are you OK?" she asked through her tears. With relief, she kissed and hugged her daughter over and over.

Stephanie lifted Cass in her arms and cried, "Good boy Cass, good boy!"

Everybody ran towards them; Mr. Johnson the crossing guard, teachers, students and lots of moms and dads.

They all shouted, "That tiny dog saved that little girl's life!"

Then something happened that Cass never expected. They began to ask,

"What's his name?"

"His name is Cass!" said Stephanie proudly. It made Cass feel proud as well.

Suddenly everyone started clapping and shouting, "Cass! Cass! Cass! Cass!"

"Cass!"

"Wow," thought Cass, "Now everybody knows my name!" Just then the principal of the Wilson Elementary School, Mr. Garcia, walked out the front door of the school. "What is going on here?" he asked.

Stepping forward Mr. Johnson said, "Cass the pug just saved the life of that little girl."

"What do you mean?" Mr. Garcia asked, "How can a dog save a little girl's life? Let's go to my office and talk about this."

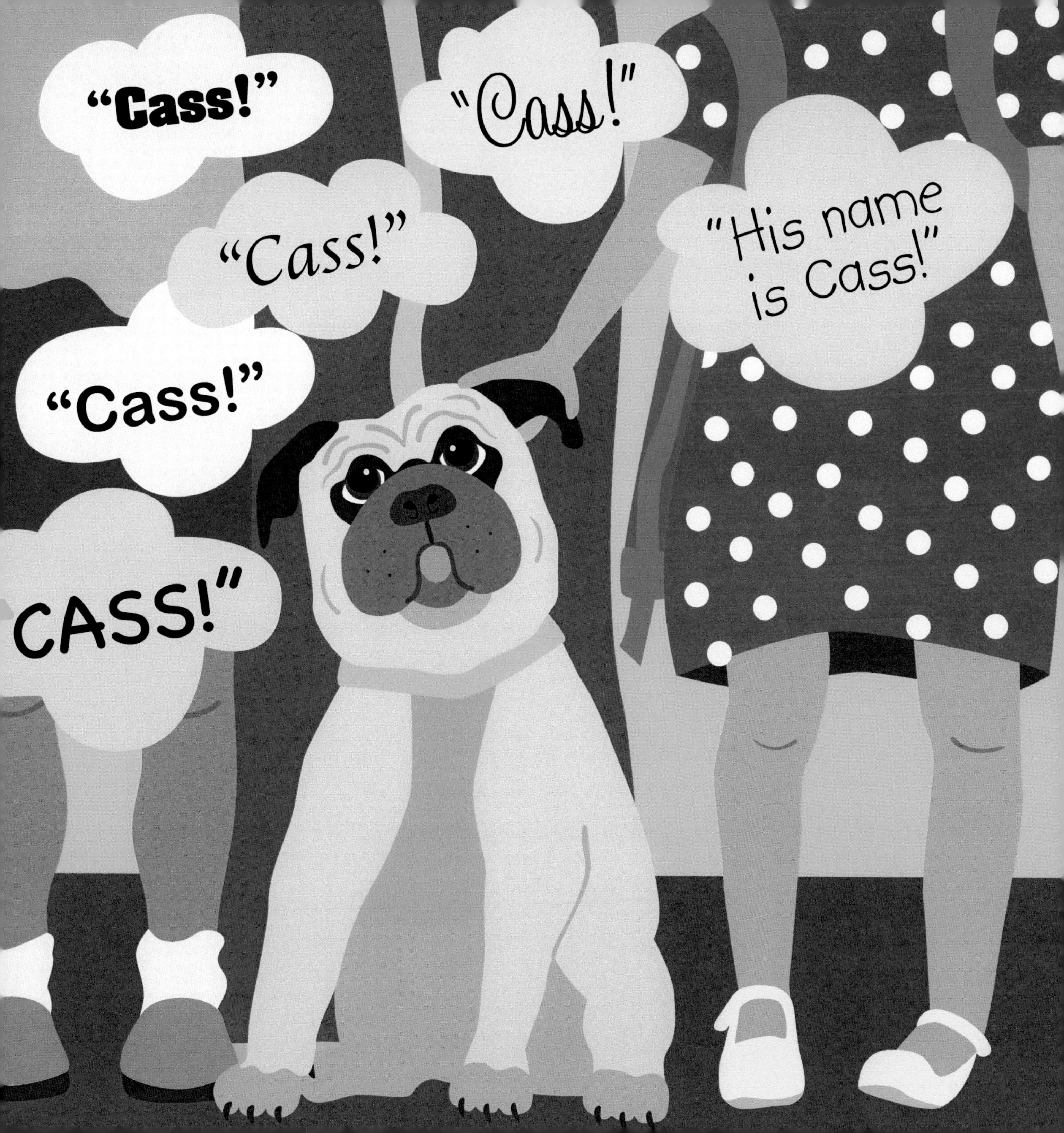
"Cass!"
"Cass!"
"Cass!"
"His name is Cass!"
"Cass!"
CASS!"

Stephanie, Cass, Mr. Johnson, the little girl and her mommy headed for the principal's office.

As Stephanie held Cass in her arms, he turned to look back at everyone. "Bye Cass! See you later Cass!" they said as they waved at him.

Stephanie held his paw and waved back. The students' clapping and shouting followed them into the school.

In the principal's office, everyone told Mr. Garcia what had happened.

They learned the little girl's name was Annie. She walked shyly over to Cass and patted him on the head. "Thank you, Cass, for saving my life," she whispered.

Cass just said, "Woof!" and everybody laughed.

Mr. Garcia said, "Cass we are going to make you an honorary member of the Wilson Elementary School. So from this day forward you are, now and forever, a member of the Wilson Elementary School student body. We are also going to make you our honorary mascot. We'll even hang a picture of you in the hallway!

Stephanie said, "Way to go Cass!"
He felt very proud.

Mr. Garcia added, "Cass, I will even call our local newspaper, *The Albuquerque Journal*, and tell them what you did."

HALL OF FAME

Wilson Elementary School

Sincerest congratulations for your outstanding implementation of programs that are enriching, enhancing and enticing your students in their pursuit of excellence in personal achievement and educational success.

DEPARTMENT OF EDUCATION

#1 State Champions

CASS

Academic Excellence

Wilson Elementary

SPELLING BEE CHAMPIONS

ALILA RAE	ZOIE LYN
TIMOTHY LON	LYDIA META
LOLA RUTH	EMILY LYNN
MIKE JOSEPH	CHRIS JAMES
LUPE CECILIA	HARLI FIONA
LYNN MEYER	NANCY RUTH
TODD LYN	GINNY JEAN
STANLEY LON	AMY JO

HONOR ROLL

- RACHEL LAUREN
- DOLORES ANNETTE
- STEPHANIE CECILIA
- PAUL JAMES
- VICTOR EUGENE
- CECILIA MARIE
- ROBERT ADRIAN
- DIEGO ANTONIO
- HORACIO HIGINIO
- PETER J.
- MARIA LOYOLA
- EVANGELINE MARTHA

• OUR HERO •

Can you imagine what happened?

The next day, Cass was on the front
page of *The Albuquerque Journal*.
The headline read,
CASS THE PUG IS A HERO!

Now, each day after breakfast
when Cass goes for a walk,
everyone greets him by name.

He is so happy to be a little
pug named Cass.

PET SECTION

Facts About Pugs

With its squashed face and wrinkled skin, the Pug is a dog with a charming appearance that appeals to many potential owners. In addition to the way it looks, it is also loved for its friendly ... and is among ... ... on ... ... aking

... ... are ... ... de a lot of ex...

The Pug has a very playful character and just wants to have fun, making them popular pets among children. They are also good around children, with the patience that is required when playing with kids. Though quite small, they are robust enough to handle the rough handling children tend to use.

Al... ... ... ire only li... ... ... ve att... ... if l... The... the... plea... poss... know... owner... wanting ... anything... The pug... companion... family, and ...

The pug makes a great companion for the whole family, and there are also some fascinating facts about them.

Ancient Pugs

The pug is an ancient breed, with some estimates dating them back 2,400 years ago. They could even be considerably older than that. Because of this, there are few details about their origins, but there are some things we do know. Pugs were bred in Tibetan monasteries by Buddhist monks, and were kept as companion dogs. There are references to a breed known as "lo-sze", and it is thought that these are ancestors of pugs, or may even have actually been pugs.

They were gifted by the monks to members of the Chinese elite, where they became very highly treasured. Western merchants then started ... ... kin ... ... West

Pugs: Everything You Need To Know

1. THEY'RE AN ANCIENT BREED.
Because the pug lineage stretches so far back, their early history is a little murky. Most believe that the breed originated in China and existed before 400 BCE and were called (or at least closely related to a breed called) "lo-sze." Buddhist monks kept the dogs as pets in Tibetan monasteries.

2. THEY WERE TREATED LIKE ROYALTY.
Emperors of China kept pugs as lapdogs and treated them to all the luxuries of royal life. Sometimes the pampered pooches were given their own mini palaces and guards.

3. A GROUP OF PUGS IS CALLED A GRUMBLE.
In Holland, the pug is called a mopshond, which comes from the Dutch for "to grumble."

4. THE BREED PROBABLY GETS ITS NAME FROM A MONKEY.
Marmosets were kept as pets in the early 18th century and were called pugs. The name made the jump to the dog because the two animals shared similar facial features.

5. THE PUG IS THE OFFICIAL BREED OF THE HOUSE OF ORANGE.
In 1572, the Dutch were in the midst of the Eighty Years' War, a protracted struggle against the Spanish. The Prince of Orange, William the Silent, led the Dutch forces into battle. According to Dutch legend, while the prince was sleeping in his tent one night, Spanish assassins lurked just outside. Luckily, William's pug, Pompey, was there to bark wildly and jump on his owner's face. The Prince woke up and had his would-be assassins apprehended. Because of this, the pug was considered the official dog of the Hou... ... nge. The effig... ... li... ... ... above his ... ... irdly, ... lieve ... ... with ...

NEW MEXICO'S LEADING NEWS SOURCE

ALBUQUERQUE JOURNAL

CASS THE PUG IS A HERO!

On an ordinary Tuesday morning Cass the Pug had gone for a walk near Wilson Elementary School with his mom, Stephanie. Suddenly, Cass noticed that a car wasn't stopping even though Mr. Johnson the crossing guard had blown his whistle. Quick as a flash, Cass broke free and rushed to save a little girl who was just about to step off the curb into the path of a speeding car. Now Cass is being honored by Mr. Garcia, principal of Wilson Elementary, as a hero. His picture is hanging in the school hall in honor of his heroic actions. Cass is only 17 pounds but he is mighty! Annie and her mom are so thankful for his quick thinking that day. Now everyone knows his name!

Cass the 17 pound pug poses for his picture which is displayed in the front hallway at Wilson Elementary School.

Cass is no ordinary pug it seems. His favorite breakfast consists of scrambled eggs, broccoli and chia seeds! He eats it every morning. He used to be a bit overweight but then his mom Stephanie put him on this special diet and he loves it. They may even create a recipe book for pugs!

Cass ... He ofte... Stephanie to ... walk each m... breakfast. He jum... up and down until she grabs his leash and off they go. They live in an apartment across the street from Wilson Elementary School. Until Cass saved little Annie's life, no one paid much attention to him which made him sad. But now it seems that everyone knows his name! He's a little 17 pound hero. Cass loves the attention! He is quick to say "woof!" in response and wag his stubby, little tail. Cass is now even more alert and watches the crosswalk carefully. He doesn't want anyone else to walk out into traffic. Mr. Johnson the crossing guard is grateful!

About the Author

Carlos Montoya lives in Albuquerque, New Mexico along with his beautiful wife Dolores, wonderful daughters Stephanie and Rachel, and cute grandson, Diego. Carlos enjoys reading, writing, history and traveling to as many places as possible. He wrote this story about his daughter Stephanie's pug named Cass because of his spunky personality and lovable nature. When Cass joined the family, Carlos became affectionately known as GPAW.

About the Illustrator

Amy Meyer Allen also lives in Albuquerque with her amazing husband Tim, sweet daughters Alila and Zoie, and spunky cats, Kiki and Karma. She loves living next to the Sandia mountains where she walks often. Amy has been drawing since she was old enough to hold a crayon. She enjoys illustrating books and doing anything creative!

Made in the USA
Monee, IL
16 May 2022

96186824R00017